A journal for teenagers experiencing a loss

Cover design by Janet Sieff, Centering Corporation
Illustrations by Ben Sieff, Centering Corporation

©1992
Centering Corporation
All rights reserved.
Revised 2003

ISBN: 1-56123-056-1
SAN: 298-1815

Additional copies and other grief resources may be ordered from:

Centering Corporation
PO Box 4600
Omaha, NE 68104

Phone: 402-553-1200
Fax: 402-553-0507

email: j1200@aol.com
online catalog: www.centering.org

Printed in Canada

Fire In My Heart, Ice In My Veins

By Enid Samuel Traisman, M.S.W.

A Note from Enid

Experiencing the death of a person you care about is probably the most painful and confusing event you ever have to face. Having it happen now, when you are already dealing with the ups and downs of being a teenager, may feel unbearable at times. You may have a lot of strong feelings, questions, concerns and opinions to sort out. It's hard to make sense of it all.

Even though there may be people around you who will listen, you may choose to keep your thoughts and feelings private. Keeping your feelings bottled up inside can make you feel even worse. This journal can be your special place to safely explore what you are going through. In this journal, you can privately record the details of your relationship, the death, your loss and the profound effect it is having on your life.

There is no right way to feel when you've suffered the death of someone you care about. Your feelings are as individual as you are and as unique as the relationship you shared. This journal has many statements reflecting the many normal thoughts and feelings teenagers experience after a loss. Every statement need not be completed, only those that strike an emotional chord in you and feel right.

It may be helpful to read through your journal in a special place where you feel safe and won't be disturbed. Sometimes you may have a lot to write, other times you may not. You may just want to doodle, or color in the illustrations while you daydream. You may write on any page that reaches you emotionally, regardless of whether it is in the beginning, middle or end of your journal. It might be helpful to date each entry so that you can look back upon your journey and see how your feelings have changed over time.

This journal is for you. It is about you and the person who died. Just reading it will let you know that all your feelings are normal, even though some may feel crazy. Writing in it will help you explore your feelings and encourage you to get them out, which is healthy for you. Writing in the journal will ensure that you will never forget.

Fire in My Heart, Ice in My Veins

Word of your death greeted me like
A wave of despair
Drowning out a bonfire of hope.

The fire in my heart,
Gave way to
The ice running through my veins.

Your death caught me from behind,
Like cold fingers gripping the back of my neck
Forcing my heart to crack open.

Your death is the fire that ravages
All through the forests of my soul,
Leaving black and grey ashes in it wake.
In the shade suddenly drawn down around,
I will plant memories of you
And inhale their sweet smell in the spring.

The fire in my heart thawed the ice running through my veins.

Life will always follow after death,
As even the longest, darkest of nights
Are followed by the light of day.

By David G. Traisman

This journal is about:

Born:

Died:

Journal Keeper:

A Very Special Person Has Died

Nobody will ever realize exactly how much you meant to me; it was just between you and me.

Amy, 15

I want to begin this journal describing who you were and what you meant to me.

Our relationship was special. Here, I'll describe things we did together, what we enjoyed, and some of our favorite things.

Our funniest time together was…

The last time we talked or saw each other was…

Some things that I remember you saying that I don't ever want to forget are...

Your Death

When I first found out that you died I was in shock, but I had to know the whole truth, every detail.
Brad, 17

This is what I know about when, where and how you died, and who was with you at the time.

My own thoughts and feelings of how and why you died:

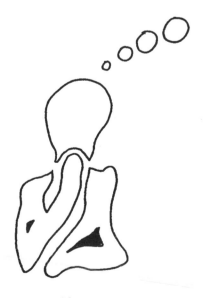

What I did and felt right after I found out about your death:

What it felt like going back to school after you died:

When I search for some meaning or try to make sense of your death, this is what I've come up with:

Sometimes I find myself imagining that if these things were different, your death might not have really happened:

I wish you could tell me what your death was like, what really happened. I think you'd say. . .

I can physically feel the pain of your death, and this is where and how I feel it in my body:

Here is a drawing of what my pain looks like...

Funeral / Memorial Service

The funeral felt so unreal, like I was watching a movie. It wasn't really us, just actors who looked like us.

Alex, 18

On this page, I will describe the funeral service, the people who spoke and the personal touches that reflected your life and personality.

This is how I felt being there (or if I didn't go, why I didn't go).

If I had planned the service for you, it would have been like this:

Sometimes I wonder what it would have been like if it was my funeral. (How would it be different?)

The funeral service handout can be attached to this page, as well as pictures and newspaper clippings.

This is what I would write on your tombstone so anyone who read it would have an idea of the person you were:

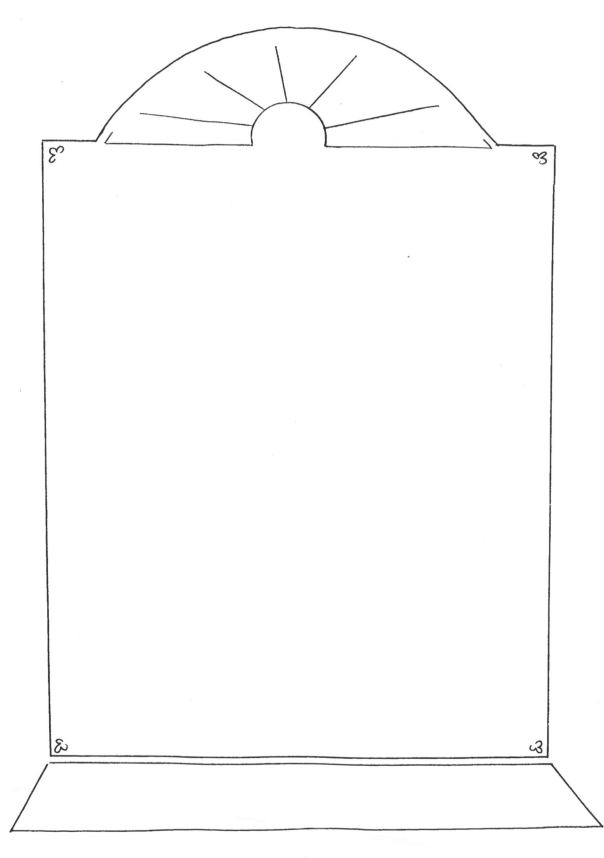

My Feelings

It seems so unfair that YOU died! It seems like other people have perfect lives, free of sadness and pain. Now I feel like I am different from most people.

Kate, 13

I feel angry!

I feel so alone…

I worry that people are judging the way I am acting. They probably think…

I think people misunderstand me because I act one way when I am feeling a different way.

Finish this picture to represent yourself.

I often wear a mask to hide what I am really feeling. I do this because. . .

Sometimes I want to run away. This is where I would like to go and why:

Sometimes I get mad and frustrated about. . .

Late at night when the world is asleep, I am awake thinking about. . .

Support

I want to talk to someone who will hear my feelings and accept them without judging or ignoring me.
If I were a small child I could get comfort easier, but I feel pressured to act more grown-up.

Jean, 15

Some family and friends have been really helpful by. . .

I feel loved and understood when. . .

Some people wanted to help but didn't know how. This is what I would have liked from them:

Some people wanted to help but I chose not to accept it because. . .

Sometimes I want to be left alone, and when I am alone I. . .

At times I just feel so angry and alone when. . .

I really want to talk to **you**. We'd help each other in these ways:

I know it's not my fault that you died, but there are some things I feel responsible for:

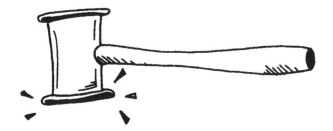

Life is different now; where do I fit in?

Letting Out the Pain -- Memorializing You

I couldn't keep my anger and sadness bottled-up inside anymore. I was afraid I would just explode! When I started writing out my difficult feelings they became less painful, and it became easier to remember happier times.

Sandy, 16

When I am involved in these activities I feel closer to you:

This symbol reminds me of you:

Physical activity really helps release stress, whether it is playing sports, dancing, jogging or taking walks. It is also a natural way to express anger. This is what I do, or will begin doing in your memory, to take care of myself:

Our friends got together and did something special in your memory:

I have kept some of your personal things. This is what I have and what they mean to me:

Music helps release feelings; here are some songs/lyrics that mean a lot to me:

A poem that I wrote, or a poem that is special:

A short story about us:

Unfinished Business

I have so many things I still want to say to my brother.

LaDonne, 14

I have some regrets and find myself going over these things that I wish I had and hadn't done:

There were some unhappy things between us that we didn't work out while you were alive. In my heart this is how I want to resolve them:

I want to tell you about these things:

There are questions I would have liked to ask you, and this is how I think you would have answered:

I wonder how you are now, what it's like, and if you are okay.

This is my goodbye letter to you:

Dreams

I love dreaming about my Grandma. When I wake up I feel like we've had a visit and that makes me feel good.

Susan, 14

A diary and dates of dreams I've had about you, some happy, some sad, and some I don't understand:

A diary and dates of some nightmares I have had:

Spiritually

When my Mom died, I began my spiritual search for the meaning of life. I am still searching.

Terry, 16

I think about the meaning of life, why people die when they do.

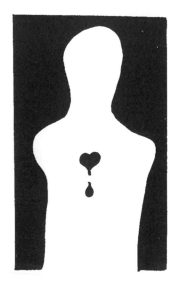

My thoughts about what happens after death and if I'll ever see you again:

There are some things I don't know the answers to:

This is what helps me find meaning in my pain over your death:

Living

Having lived through my twin's death has changed my life in many ways. One way: being that since I have lived through this I am strong enough to handle anything.

Evan, 19

When you died, I thought I could not go on. I had to because...

My life is important; I have many things to look forward to:

The biggest challenges I continue to face are . . .

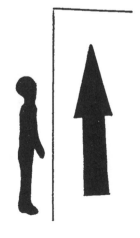

Your life and death have changed me and have changed the following priorities in my life:

Things I was never aware of before, but am aware of now:

I now recognize the following strengths in myself:

The most important things I've learned since your death are. . .

The Future Without You

These special events won't be the same without your physical presence, but I will do something special to include you.

Aaron, 17

This is how the event would have been different if you had been here too:

Birthdays:

School graduations:

Marriage:

Birth of my children:

Holidays:

Other significant events:

Thoughts

Thoughts

Pictures, Photographs, Etc.

About the Author

Enid Samuel Traisman, M.S.W., is a therapist specializing in bereavement and loss in Portland, Oregon. She facilitates grief support groups, conducts a part-time private practice and presents seminars to caregivers and grieving people. Enid is also the author of *I Remember, I Remember*, a journal for adults, *A Child Remembers*, a journal for children ages 8-12, and *My Personal Pet Remembrance Journal*.

Special thanks to Centering Corporation and Ben and Janet Sieff;
especially Janet for her wonderful ideas and endless enthusiasm.

To David, my husband, for his beautiful poem and his support.

And to the Dougy Center for Grieving Children and their grieving children.
The caring feedback about the contents of this journal was helpful and deeply appreciated.